What am I?
The Winter Games

Today's Events

Ice hockey	Freestyle skiing
Cross-country skiing	Ski jumping
Curling	Luge
Bobsled	Speed skating
Downhill skiing	Snowboarding
Figure skating	Skeleton
Biathlon	Ski mountaineering

I am a variety of sporting events
played during the winter.

I have some riddles for you,
curious reader,
to figure out
what events I am.

Bobsledding? Skiing? Curling?

Turn the page to start guessing.
If you guess each event correctly,
you'll win a gold medal!

I'm a game played on ice
on a rectangular frozen rink.

With sticks and a puck
players skate around,
trying to score a goal.

The game may be rough
with hard body checks,
while intense power plays
and face-offs add to the fun.

At the end of three periods,
the buzzer signals the end.
The team with the most goals wins.

What am I?

ICE HOCKEY

I'm an outdoor sport held across
snowy fields and hills;
A race course in the wilderness.

Skis swish and swoosh
as they cross over fluffy snow,
around turns and curves.

Sprints, relays,
and marathon events challenge
athletes to go the distance
to the finish line.

What am I?

I'm held on a long sheet of ice,
a target on each end.

A circular stone of polished granite
is delivered down the ice,
aimed for the center of the target.

Players use special brushes
to guide a stone across the ice,
controlling its speed and rotation.

Teams use special tactics to block
or tap their opponent's stones
to prevent them from scoring.

The team that gets its stones
as close as possible
to the center point wins points.

What am I?

I'm a fast-paced race
down an icy, narrow race track.

The running push-off at the start
propels crews forward down the ice,
faster and faster they go.

Teams pilot sleds downhill,
zooming around sharp banks,
quick curves and turns,
a thrilling ride to the finish.

The fastest team is declared
the winner.

What am I?

I'm a speedy sport,
racing down a snow-covered
mountain slope,
a race against the clock.

Athletes on skis zoom
around poles or gates,
turning quickly in their sprint
to the finish.

Slalom and giant slalom,
super-G, and downhill are
all events in this
fast-paced, technical sport.

What am I?

On an ice rink I'm held,
for ice skates are a must,
to perform this graceful event.

Competitors skate
in loops and twirls,
a set of figures or patterns
across the chilled ice.

Often, with music or a partner,
spins, jumps, and steps
turn ice skating into an
artistic dance.

What am I?

I'm a two-part contest,
a combination of
speed and precision.

Across snowy trails
athletes race on skis,
carrying rifles on their backs.

Then, at shooting ranges,
athletes shoot at five targets
from a standing or lying position.

Skill and accuracy are important,
for if a target is missed,
a time or distance
penalty is added.

What am I?

I'm an adrenaline-fueled sport
of wild stunts,
breathtaking jumps,
and crazy acrobatics,
all performed on snow skis.

In aerials, skiers launch into the air,
performing twists and flips,
before landing back on the ground.

In moguls, skiers speed across bumpy
snow mounds with technique and skill.

Ski cross forces competitors together,
facing jumps and high banked turns.

Halfpipe and slopestyle involve
elaborate tricks on a half-pipe
or on beams and jumps.

With a fun, free style
athletes add their own touch
to these events.

What am I?

FREESTYLE SKIING

I'm a gravity-defying event
that uses long, wide skis
for stability and lift.

Athletes speed down
a curved jump ramp
to take flight at the end,
soaring as far as possible
down a hill to the k-point
at the bottom.

Jumping techniques
such as parallel or v-style
help jumpers fly through the air,
as they maintain poise
and balance before landing.

What am I?

SKI JUMPING

I'm the fastest race on ice,
sliding down an icy track
on a little sled.

Racers lie on their backs,
face up and feet first,
as they speed down the raceway,
hurdling around curves
and zipping around tight corners.

Athletes steer at high speeds
by slight movements
of their shoulders and torso
to be the fastest to the finish line.

What am I?

I'm an indoor sport,
held on an oval ice track,
a sprint against the clock
for the fastest time.

Cruising across ice
with special clap skates,
athletes race in pairs
over varying distances.

Short track racing
with mass starts
offers a different format
for competitors to race against
each other for first place.

What am I?

I'm a fun sport
that uses neither skis nor skates
but special boards,
skateboards on the snow.

Some events focus on
freestyle tricks,
where riders perform
jumps, spins, and flips
on half pipes,
obstacles, or on a big jump
where style wins points.

Other races
involve riders speeding
through an obstacle course,
leaping over jumps and bumps,
trying to be the fastest.

What am I?

SNOWBOARDING

I'm another sliding sport,
similar to the luge,
where athletes lie
face down and head first,
almost one in body and sled.

With a quick sprint,
racers leap onto a sled,
then speed through an icy track,
reaching high speeds as they
zoom around tight turns
and dangerous curves
as they rocket to the finish.

What am I?

SKELETON

I'm an outdoor sport
held in the mountains,
over snowy, challenging terrain.

Athletes race across a course,
beginning with a climb up
a mountain on skis,
then ascending higher on foot.

Finally, racers ski downhill
as they navigate a rugged terrain,
speeding to the finish.

What am I?

What am I? The Winter Games

Copyright © 2026 by John Benzee
All illustrations and text by John Benzee

All rights reserved.
No part of this book may be used or reproduced in any manner whatsoever without permission, except in the case of brief quotations in critical articles or reviews.
Any use of this publication to "train" generative artificial intelligence (AI) technologies to generate text or illustrations is expressly prohibited.

Published by Split Seed Press; Clarence, NY
ISBN: 978-0-9997379-7-2 (hardcover)
ISBN: 978-0-9997379-8-9 (paperback)

First edition
Library of Congress Control Number: 2025921030

Visit johnbenzee.com for more information

Typeset in Roboto. Illustrations created in Procreate & Affinity Designer.

Publisher's Cataloging-In-Publication Data:
Names: Benzee, John, 1995— author, illustrator.
Title: What am I? The Winter Games / by John Benzee.
Description: Clarence, NY : Split Seed Press, 2026. | Series: What am I? series. | Summary: A series of riddles that give descriptions of Winter Olympic sports and then reveal their names.
Identifiers: ISBN 9780999737972 (hardcover) | ISBN 9780999737989 (paperback)
Subjects: LCSH: Winter sports—Winter Olympics—Juvenile literature. | Riddles, Juvenile.
Classification: GV841.5.B46 2026 | DDC 796.98--dc23

10 9 8 7 6 5 4 3 2 1

www.ingramcontent.com/pod-product-compliance
Lightning Source LLC
Chambersburg PA
CBHW052046070526
44584CB00018B/2628